Prayer

and # Wisdom

A COLLECTION OF LEARNINGS

Prayer *and* Wisdom

A COLLECTION OF LEARNINGS

DENNIS R. MALLY

ISBN 0-9727318-0-6

Topanga Publishing
PO Box 535
Coloma, Michigan 49038-0535
info@topangapublishing.com
www.topangapublishing.com

Printed in the United States of America
LithoTech Graphic Services

Cover design by Robin Costa Booth
Cover photo by Dennis Mally
Photo of the author by Antonina Mally

To All Those Who Formed Me

God, Antonina, Mom and Dad,
My Children, Grandchildren,
Brothers and Sisters, Relatives, Friends,
Professors, Teachers, Students,
Nuns, Priests, Retreatants,
Preachers, Worshippers, Choir Members,
Managers, Supervisors,
Partners, Subordinates, Secretaries,
Associates, Team Members, Board Members,
Neighbors, Club Members,
Customers, Suppliers, Sales Persons,
Shop Keepers, Business Owners,
Receptionists, Doctors, Nurses,
Reporters, Authors, Columnists, Writers,
Politicians, Comedians,
Composers, Artists, Performers,
Singers, Musicians,
Radio and Television Talkers,
Actors, Actresses, Directors, Producers,
Waiters, Cooks, Cashiers,
Bus Drivers, Taxi Drivers,
Delivery Men, Installers,
Vagrants, Panhandlers

Contents

From the Author

Dear Friend,

I thought I should begin with a few words about how and why this little book came to be written.

In the basement of our house, stashed away in one of the many boxes of stuff a basement collects, is a large red scrapbook. It has a faux leather cover with gold embossed trim and two eyelets laced with black shoestring that bind the covers and pages together. Written in gold ink in the lower right corner is "Scrap Book," just so there is no doubt what it is. Inside, the buff colored construction-paper pages are nearly filled with neatly cut and pasted clippings from old Detroit newspapers and Look magazine. If the item (i.e., picture) wasn't about sports, it wasn't included. Baseball, football, hockey, pro, college and high school are all covered in no particular order. Page one is taken up with a full-color photo of Bob "Hunchy" Hoernschemyer, star Lions' halfback posing in his blue and white jersey and faceguard-less helmet, prior to the start of the 1952-3 season. Near the end of the red scrapbook, in front of a few blank pages, is a torn-out but never pasted-in series of

"Know Your 1953 Tigers" articles from the now long defunct Detroit Times.

I formed the habit of clipping and collecting at an early age — ten, and unbeknownst to anyone, those loose clippings that were stuffed into the back of my childhood scrapbook were the foreshadowing of a book to come.

On July 11, 1960 I began my career as a co-operative engineering student, alternating between work at Cadillac Motor Car (as it was called then) and school terms at General Motors Institute (as it was called then). On December 1, 2000, I retired from the Wm. Wrigley Jr. Company as Vice President - Information Services. Between those two events I encountered many good and wise people and a gold-mine of learning opportunities.

I worked for and with many different organizations, in different departments and functions, and in many different capacities. I met thousands of people. Attended countless meetings, seminars, and conferences. Read innumerable books, magazines, reports, letters and memos. Listened to countless radio programs, and audiotapes and watched many hundreds of hours of television. I attended thousands of church services, religious retreats, weddings and funerals. I wrote. I thought. I talked. I contemplated. And throughout this journey I was learning . . . and clipping, and saving.

Anytime I heard or saw or thought something that contributed to my growth — a profound bit of wisdom, a penetrating touch of humor, a fundamental truth, or a meaningful prayer — I retained it. Some items were written down and dropped into a file folder. Others were stored in my memory. Over the years, as I grew, the collection grew. And, not surprisingly, it evolved into a reasonably good abstract of my core values and fundamental beliefs.

Earlier this year, about a year after my retirement, I took up the question of what to do with this collection. The boxes in the basement and my memory banks were begging to be cleaned out. After evaluating several alternatives I came upon the obvious. I decided that I would gather them into a book — a Scrap Book!

So here it is, my scrapbook of learnings; bits of wisdom and prayer gathered over 40 years of work and play, suffering and joy. I share them with you now with the hope that you will find among them at least a few things that inspire, enlighten or amuse you. Enjoy.

Best regards,

.

Prayer and Wisdom

Prayer of St. Francis

Lord, make me an instrument of your peace.
Where there is hatred, let me sow love.
Where there is injury, pardon.
Where there is doubt, faith.
Where there is despair, hope.
Where there is darkness, light.
And where there is sadness, joy.

O Divine Master, grant that I may not so much
seek to be consoled as to console,
to be understood as to understand,
to be loved as to love.
For it is in giving that we receive.
It is in pardoning that we are pardoned.
And it is in dying that we are born to eternal life.

— St. Francis of Assisi

Intuition
You always know more than you can prove.
— *Jewish proverb*

As A Man Thinketh
A man's mind may be likened to a garden, which may be intelligently cultivated or allowed to run wild; but whether cultivated or neglected, it must, and will, bring forth.
— *James Allen*

Greed
Bulls make money. Bears make money. Pigs get slaughtered.
— *Jim Cramer*

Perspective
Two men looked out from prison bars. One saw mud; one saw stars.
— *Anonymous*

Golden Rule
Treat others the way you would have them
treat you.

— Mt 7:12, Lk 6:31

Gossip
You can't build yourself up by tearing someone
else down.

— DRM

Through the Eyes . . .
Nothing would ever get done around here
without me.

— Dominic LaRocca (4 yrs)

Ambition
You can do anything in the world you like, as long
as you're willing to pay the price.

— Jim McKelvey

Peace of Mind

Do not look forward to what might happen
tomorrow; the same everlasting Father who cares
for you today, will take care of you tomorrow,
and every day. Either He will shield you from
suffering or He will give you unfailing strength
to bear it.

Be at peace then, and put aside all anxious thoughts
and imaginations.

— St. Francis DeSales

Common Sense

Common sense is not so common.

— Voltaire

Heart Memory

What the heart has once owned and had, it shall
never lose.

— Henry Ward Beecher

Laws of Nature

"I remember one morning when I discovered a cocoon in the bark of a tree, just as a butterfly was making a hole in its case and preparing to come out. I waited a while, but it was too long appearing and I was impatient. I bent over it and breathed on it to warm it. I warmed it as quickly as I could and the miracle began to happen before my eyes, faster than life. The case opened, the butterfly started slowly crawling out and I shall never forget my horror when I saw how its wings were folded back and crumpled; the wretched butterfly tried with its whole trembling body to unfold them. Bending over it, I tried to help it with my breath; in vain.

It needed to be hatched out patiently and the unfolding of the wings should be a gradual process in the sun. Now it was too late. My breath had forced the butterfly to appear, all crumpled, before its time. It struggled desperately and, a few seconds later, died in the palm of my hand.

The little boy is, I do believe, the greatest weight I have on my conscience. For I realize today that it is a mortal sin to violate the great laws of nature. We should not hurry, we should not be impatient, but we should confidently obey the eternal rhythm."
    — *"Zorba The Greek," by Kazantzakis*

Problems?
Insurmountable "Opportunities"

— *Bill Skimin*

Friendship
Friendship blossoms, grows and is strengthened in the measure that virtue develops.

— *St. Thomas Aquinas*

Serenity Prayer
God, grant me the serenity
To accept the things I cannot change,
The courage to change the things I can, and
The wisdom to know the difference.

— *Anonymous*

Speeches/Presentations
Your audience doesn't know as much as you think they do.

— *John F. Bard*

Fully Human, Fully Alive
Our participation in the happiness of a full and human life is determined by our personal perception of reality.

— Rev John Powell, S.J.

Great Works
Genius begins great works; labor alone finishes them.

— Joseph Joubert

Facts
Facts are stubborn things.

— Rene Le Sage

Success
The talent of success is nothing more than doing what you can do well and doing well whatever you do.

— Longfellow

Raising Children

When children live with criticism they learn to
condemn.
When children live with hostility, they learn to
fight.
When children live with ridicule, they learn to
be shy.
When children live with shame, they learn to
feel guilty.
When children live with tolerance, they learn to
be patient.
When children live with encouragement, they
learn confidence.
When children live with security, they learn to
have faith.
When children live with fairness, they learn
justice.
When children live with praise, they learn to
appreciate.
When children live with approval, they learn to
like themselves.
When children live with acceptance and
friendship;
They learn to find love in the World.

— *Linda Knowles*

Job Perspective
Never forget that the people who work for you
have a worse job than yours.

— Dale Dauten

Stress Relief
Come by yourselves to an out-of-the-way place
and rest a little.

— Mk 6:30

Planning
If you don't know where you're going you'll end up
somewhere else.

— Yogi Berra

Setting Example
It is good to teach, if we practice what we preach.

— St. Ignatius of Antioch

Leaders

Men who know not, and know not that they know
   not, are fools. Shun them.
Men who know not, and know that they know not,
   are simpletons. Teach them.
Men who know, and know not that they know,
are sleepers. Wake them.
Men who know, and know that they know, are wise.
   Follow them.

— Arabian Proverb

Accepting Responsibility

If the truth hurts, "wear" it.

— DRM

Associates

Seek the association of persons who are good,
for if you are the companion of their life,
you will also be the companion of their virtue.

— St. Isidore

Perseverance

He who runs from a difficulty must face two.

— *"Safe Methods of Business"*, © *1886*

Honesty

No legacy is so rich as honesty.

— *William Shakespeare*

Like and Love

You like somebody *because*. You love somebody *despite*.

— *Rev Bob Morin, OMI*

Righting Wrongs

It is never too late, nor is it too early to get started on something that needs doing.

— *DRM*

Communication

Seek first to be understood, then to understand.

— Stephen R. Covey

An Irish Blessing

May love and warmth always surround you in
    your home.
May the peace of Christ abide in you wherever
    you may roam.
May the blessing of light be upon you,
    light without and light within.
May the wisdom of heaven guide you until
    we meet again.

— Anonymous

Sharing Credit

There is no limit to what a man can do or where
he can go if he doesn't mind who gets the credit.

— Anonymous
Posted on President Reagan's Oval Office Desk

Positive Thinking

Whether you think you *can*, or think you *can't* . . .
you're right.

— *Henry Ford*

Attitude

The longer I live, the more I realize the impact
of attitude on life. Attitude, to me, is more
important than facts. It is more important than
the past, than education, than money, than circum-
stances, than failures, than successes, than what
other people think or say or do. It is more important than appearance, giftedness or skill. It will
make or break a company, a church, a home,
a person. The remarkable thing is, you have a choice
every day regarding the attitude you will embrace
for that day. We cannot change our past. We cannot
change the fact that people will think or act in
a certain way. We cannot change the inevitable.
The only thing we can do is play on the one string
we have, and that is our *attitude*. I am convinced
that life is 10% what happens to me and 90% how
I react to it. And so it is with you.

— *Charles Swindoll*

Outcomes

If you only do what you've always done, then you
only get what you already have.

— Anonymous

Dreams

What happens to a dream deferred?
Does it dry up
Like a raisin in the sun?
Or fester like a sore —-
And then run?
Does it stink like rotten meat
or crust and sugar over —-
Like a syrupy sweet?

Maybe it just sags
like a heavy load.

Or does it explode?

— Langston Hughes

Leadership
Actions speak louder than speeches.

— James X. Mullen

Love
Let us love in deed and in truth and not merely talk about it.

— 1 Jn 3:18

Surveys
Ask enough people for their opinion, and they will, on average, recommend being average.

— Dale Dauten

Suffering
Suffering is like a kiss that Jesus hanging from the Cross bestows on persons He loves in a special way. Because of this love He wants to associate them in the work of the Redemption.

— St. Bonaventure

Introspection
The unexamined life is not worth living.

— Socrates

Youth
Youth is not a time of life; it is a state of mind;
it is not a matter of rosy cheeks, red lips and
supple knees; it is a matter of will, a quality of
the imagination, a vigor of the emotions; it is
the freshness of the deep springs of life.

Youth means a temperamental predominance of
courage over timidity of the appetite, for adventure
over the love of ease. This often exists in a man
of 60 more than a boy of 20. Nobody grows old
merely by a number of years. We grow old by
deserting our ideals.

Years may wrinkle the skin, but to give up
enthusiasm wrinkles the soul. Worry, fear,
self-distrust bows the heart and turns the
spirit back to dust.

Whether 60 or 16, there is in every human being's heart the lure of wonder, the unfailing childlike appetite of what's next and the joy of the game of living. In the center of your heart and my heart there is a wireless station: so long as it receives messages of beauty, hope, cheer, courage and power from men and from God, so long are you young.

When aerials are down, and your spirit is covered with snows of cynicism and the ice of pessimism, then you are grown old, even at 20. But as long as your aerials are up, to catch waves of optimism, there is hope you may die young at 90.

— *Samuel Ullman*

Career Planning

We do well what we enjoy doing, and enjoy doing what we do well.

— *Anonymous/DRM*

Money
Whether you have a little or a lot, you never
have enough.

— Frank J. Babel

Faith
Whatever you ask for in prayer, with faith,
you will receive.

— Matt 21:22

Integrity
Integrity is DWYSYWD, doing what you said
you would do.

— DRM

Time Management
Something that isn't worth doing isn't worth
doing well.

— Sal Marino

Life's Problems
There are only two real disasters in life: one is
to have an aspiration that is never granted,
while the other is to have a great dream that is
actually fulfilled.

— Proverb

Motivating Employees
Pay more, expect more.

— Dale Dauten

Friends
Everyone hears what you say. Friends listen
to what you say. Best friends listen to what
you don't say.

— Tim McGraw

Politics
Politics is supposed to be the second oldest
profession. I have come to realize that it bears
a very close resemblance to the first.

— Ronald Reagan

Career Advice For The Young

Know your strength. The most important thing
is to know what you're good at. Very few people
know that. All of us know what we're not good at.
But the reason why so few of us know what we're
good at is that it comes so easy. You sweat over
what's hard to do. So knowing what you're good
at is the first thing.

The second thing is to know when to change.
There are certain situations in which you don't stay.
You don't stay in a situation that corrupts.
Better to go off the diving board on your own,
even if you're not sure there's water down there.
And know when to quit. If you're no longer learning
anything, if your work no longer challenges you,
if you feel "I've only got twenty years to retirement,"
then get out.

— *Peter Drucker*

Success

The secret of success is constancy to purpose.

— *Benjamin Disraeli*

Success

There are really only three keys to success in Business: Show up on time. Return your phone calls. Do a good job.

— *John R. Brandt*

Open Mind

The fellow with a closed mind is usually the one with the open mouth.

— *Anonymous*

Management/Leadership

There's no way you can run an operation if you're going to try to make it through love. The leader has to be the one they dislike.

— *Sparky Anderson*

Ideas

An invasion of armies can be resisted, but not an idea whose time has come.

— *Victor Hugo*

Take Some Time

Take some time to smell the flowers
　　as you walk the paths of life.
Take some time to ease the tensions
　　from the challenges and strife.

Take some time to hear the birds sing
　　as they usher in the dawn.
Though the day be just emerging,
　　too soon it will be gone.

Take some time to watch a sunrise,
　　now and then a sunset too.
Just be sure that seeking pleasure
　　isn't all you ever do.

Take some time to count your blessings,
　　though you feel they're not that great.
You will find they're more abundant
　　than you thought, at any rate.

Take some time to banish hatred
　　when and where you can.
Just detest man's evil ways
　　and not your fellow man.

Take some time to love your children
    every moment you are free.
The benefits exceedeth
    a university degree.

Take some time to love your neighbor
    and even more important still,
Take some time to love yourself
    or not many others will.

And if you don't like that image
    of yourself that others see
Take some time to make some changes.
    Be the best that you can be.

Take some time to live by virtue
    in the best way that is known,
And respect the rights of others
    as equal to your own.

Take some time to just appreciate
    the fact that you are here,
And to know that Higher Power
    and to trust it without fear.

If you do these things with diligence
    you will eventually be glad.
If you don't attempt to do them
    you may one day wish you had.

Although this no doubt could impose
     upon your time for seeking wealth,
There should be little question
     that it could improve your health.

And though you might not be as wealthy,
     nor drive so fine a car,
You'll find you will be richer
     in other ways by far.

— Leon Hansen

Life Directions

"Would you tell me please, which way I ought to go
from here?" "That depends a good deal on where
you want to get to," said the cat.

— "Alice In Wonderland", by Louis Carroll

Faith

The Apostles said to the Lord, "Increase our Faith,"
and he answered: "If you had faith the size of
a mustard seed, you could say to this sycamore,
'Be uprooted and transplanted into the sea,'
and it would obey you."

— Lk 17:5-6

Business Management
Managers are not obligated to perpetuate
foolishness.

— EDS Leadership Conference

Getting and Giving
What we are is God's gift to us.
What we become is our gift to God.

— Anonymous

A Daily Prayer
Jesus, Good Shepherd,
I place myself in your hands today,
All of my work and play,
Suffering and joy.
Guide me, and all I love.
Keep us safe from harm and bring us safely
home to You.

— Anonymous

It Couldn't Be Done

Somebody said that it couldn't be done,
But he with a chuckle replied
That "maybe it couldn't," but he would be one
Who wouldn't say so till he tried.
So he buckled right in with the trace of a grin
On his face. If he worried he hid it.
He started to sing as he tackled the thing
That couldn't be done, and he did it.

Somebody scoffed: "Oh, you'll never do that;
At least no one ever has done it."
But he took off his coat and he took off his hat,
And the first thing we knew he'd begun it.
With a lift of his chin and a bit of a grin,
Without any doubting or quiddit,
He started to sing as he tackled the thing
That couldn't be done, and he did it.

There are thousands to tell you it cannot be done,
There are thousands to prophesy failure.
There are thousands to point out to you one by one,
The dangers that wait to assail you.
But just buckle in with a bit of a grin,
Just take off your coat and go to it.
Just start in to sing as you tackle the thing
That "cannot be done," and you'll do it.

— *Edgar A. Guest*

Teaching
Never try to teach a pig to sing.
It wastes your time and annoys the pig.

— *Anonymous*

"I . . ."
What you *did* matters less than what you *do*.

— *DRM*

Status
The value of our life does not depend on the place
we occupy. It depends on the way we occupy
that place.

— *St. Theresa of the Child Jesus*

Ability
Ability is a poor man's wealth.

— *Wren*

Tools

A man who needs a tool and doesn't have it,
is paying for the tool whether he has it or not.

— *John Patterson*

Peace of Mind

Let go and let God.

— *Rev Patrick Brennan, C.P.*

Nice Person?

A person who is nice to you but rude to the waiter
is not a nice person.

— *Dave Berry*

Management/Leadership

Management is getting people to do what needs
to be done. Leadership is getting people to want
to do what needs to be done.

— *Warren Bennis*

Success

What is success?

To laugh often and much;

To win the respect of intelligent people and the affection of children;

To earn the appreciation of honest critics and endure the betrayal of false friends;

To appreciate beauty;

To find the best in others;

To leave the world a bit better, whether by a healthy child, a garden patch or a redeemed social condition;

To know even one life has breathed easier because you have lived;

This is to have succeeded.

— *Ralph Waldo Emerson*

Verbal Diarrhea

"Driving this hack has taught me that there ain't no proof a guy's tongue is attached to his brain."

— New York Cab Driver

Hiring Employees

I just don't want bad people. I don't like bad people.

— Sparky Anderson

Prayer For Forgiveness

Have mercy on us, God, in your kindness. Save us and restore us to your friendship. Look upon our contrite heart and sorrowful spirit and heal our troubled conscience, so that in the joy and strength of the Holy Spirit we may proclaim your praise and glory.

— Anonymous

Be Yourself

Don't seek to live somebody else's life;
it's just not for you . . .
You have no right to put on a false face,
to pretend you're what you're not,
unless you want to rob others.
Say to yourself:
I am going to bring something new
into this person's life,
because he has never met anyone like me,
for in the mind of God
I am unique and irreplaceable.

— *Michel Quoist*

Employee Relations

Your employees will treat your customers only
as well as they are treated.

— *Anonymous*

Rumors

A lie can travel halfway around the world while
the truth is putting on its shoes.

— *Mark Twain*

Heroism

To be a hero for a moment, for an hour,
is easier than to bear the heroism of everyday life.
Accepting life as it is – gray and monotonous,
accepting that activity for which no one praises you,
that heroism which no one notes, which draws
no attention to yourself . . . he who bears that
colorless challenge of life and still remains strong
is indeed a hero!

— Feodor Dostoyevsky

Caveat Emptor

When the fox preaches beware of your geese.

— "Safe Methods of Business", © 1886

Influence

Men do not attract that which they *want*, but
that which they *are*.

— James Allen

Love Me Now

If you are ever going to love me,
Love me now, while I can know
The sweet and tender feelings
Which from true affection flow.
Love me now
While I am living.
Do not wait until I'm gone
And then have it chiseled in marble,
Sweet words on ice-cold stone.
If you have tender thoughts of me,
Please tell me now.
If you wait until I am sleeping,
Never to awaken,
There will be death between us,
And I won't hear you then.
So, if you love me, even a little bit,
Let me know it while I'm living
So I can treasure it.

— Anonymous

Heaven's Price

Give yourself and it is enough. For the merciful
Lord is satisfied with that.

— St. Augustine

Precious Time

God puts 86,400 seconds in your account every day. Use it well while you have it. Anything you do not use will not be carried over.

To realize the value of one *year,* ask a student who has failed his final exam.

One *month*? Ask a mother who has given birth to a premature baby.

One *week*? Ask an editor of a weekly newspaper.

One *hour*? Ask the lovers who are waiting to meet.

One *minute*? Ask a person who has missed the train.

One *second*? Ask a person who has survived an accident.

One *millisecond*? Ask the person who has won a silver medal in the Olympics.

To find the value of one *lifetime* ask someone who has missed their chance.

— *John Black*

Life

What is it all, when all is told,
This constant striving for fame or gold,
The fleeting joys, the bitter tears?
We are only here a few short years.
Nothing our own but the silent past,
Loving or hating, nothing can last!
What is it all, but a passing through,
A cross for me and a cross for you?
Ours seems heavy, while others seem light,
But God in the end, makes all things right!
He tempers the wind with such loving care,
He knows the burdens each can bear,
Then he changes life's gray into heavenly gold.
Ah! That is all, when all is told!

— *Anonymous*

Teaching

Tell me, and I'll forget.
Show me, and I'll remember.
Involve me, and I'll understand.

— *B. Lee Tuttle, GMI Professor*

Native American Prayer

Oh great Spirit whose voice I hear in the winds,
and whose breath gives life to all the world, hear
me! I am small and weak; I need your strength
and wisdom.

Let me walk in beauty, and make my eyes ever
behold the red and purple sunset.

Make my hands respect the things you have made
and my ears sharp to hear your voice.

Make me wise so that I may understand the things
you have taught my people.

Let me learn the lessons you have hidden in every
leaf and rock.

I seek strength, not to be greater than my brother,
but to fight my greatest enemy – myself.

Make me always ready to come to you with clean
hands and straight eyes.

So when life fades, as the fading sunset, my spirit
may come to you without shame.

— Anonymous

Criticism

Make it *instructive* if you want it to be constructive.

— DRM

Simplicity

'Tis a gift to be simple.
'Tis a gift to be free,
'Tis a gift to come down
where you ought to be.

— Quaker hymn

Gaelic Blessing

May the road rise up to meet you.
May the wind be always at your back.
May the sun shine warm upon your face;
The rains fall soft upon your fields.
And, until we meet again,
May the good Lord hold you in the palm
of his hand.

— Anonymous

Risk

To laugh is to risk appearing the fool.
To weep is to risk appearing sentimental.
To reach out for another is to risk involvement.
To expose feelings is to risk exposing your self.
To place your ideas, your dreams before the crowds
is to risk their loss.
To love is to risk not being loved in return.
To live is to risk dying.
To hope is to risk despair.
To try is to risk failure.

But risks must be taken because the greatest hazard
in life is to risk nothing.
The person who risks nothing, does nothing,
has nothing; is nothing.
She may avoid suffering and sorrow, but she simply
cannot learn, feel, change, grow, live, love, live.
Chained by her certitude, she is a slave;
she has forfeited her freedom.

Only a person who risks is free.

— *Anonymous*

Sonnet XXIX

When, in disgrace with Fortune and men's eyes,
I all alone beweep my outcast state
And trouble deaf heaven with my bootless cries
And look upon myself and curse my fate,
Wishing me like to one more rich in hope,
Featured like him, like him with friends possess'd,
Desiring this man's art and that man's scope,
With what I most enjoy contented least;
Yet in these thoughts myself almost despising,
Haply I think on thee, and then my state,
Like to the lark at break of day arising
From sullen earth, sings hymns at heaven's gate;
For thy sweet love remember'd such wealth brings
That then I scorn to change my state with kings.

— *William Shakespeare*

The Dark Forest

You can only go halfway into the darkest forest;
then you are coming out the other side.

> —*Chinese Proverb*

Carpe Diem

Regard every day as if you are then beginning
for the first time. And always act with the same
fervor that you had on the first day you began.

> — *St. Anthony of Padua*
> — *Title: Seize the Day, from the movie "Dead Poets Society"*

Can Do

Eliminate "I can't" from your vocabulary.

> — *Richard "Buzz" Brescoll*

Habits

We begin by making habits and end by habits
making us.

> — *Anonymous*

Job Performance
There are darn few bad workers, but many bad
job fits.

— *DRM*

Love
It's love that makes the bright days a little
brighter yet.
It's love that makes the memories too precious
to forget.
It's love that makes the love of life so wonderful
to share.
It's love that keeps hearts caring through happiness
and tears.
Rewarding those who share it with rich and
happy years.
And though time may bring its changes the way
it always will,
True love, with time, grows deeper —
True love grows sweeter still.

— *Anonymous/Antonina*

Time Management
You may delay, but time will not.

— *Ben Franklin*

The Good Life
To discover the good life, look to the dimensions
within you that harbor truth, absorb the beauty
around you, help others and love another.

— *Fr. Eugene Hemrick*

Behavior
Human behavior is goal directed — theirs,
not yours.

— *Main Event Management*

Love
Love is the source of all good things.

— *St. Fulgentius*

Parable of The True Friend

A man is walking down a street and he falls into
a deep hole. The sides are steep and slippery.
He can't get out.

He looks up from his trap and sees that a Doctor
is walking by. So he calls up to him for help.
The doctor takes out a pen and pad, writes
a prescription, tosses it down to the man and
walks on.

A little while later a Minister walks by and once
again the man calls up, "hey Reverend, can you
help me?" The minister takes out his pen, writes
a prayer, tosses it down to the man and walks on.

Still later a Friend walks by. The man recognizes
him and calls up and asks for his help. Without
hesitation, the friend jumps into the hole! The man
says, "What the hell are you doing? How dumb
was that? Now we're both stuck down here."

The friend replies, "Yes, I hear you. But I've been
down here before and I know the way out."

— From "West Wing", a TV series

Conscience

Hold fast to . . . a good conscience. Some men,
by rejecting the guidance of conscience, have made
shipwrecks of their faith.

— 1 Tim 1:19

Problem-solving

Kill "snakes", not time.

— Ross Perot/DRM

Reality

If it seems too good to be true, it's probably
not true.

— Anonymous

Child Rearing

It is easier to build a child than to repair an adult.

— Cheerios Box Top

Helping Others

You cannot bring about prosperity by discouraging thrift.

You cannot strengthen the weak by weakening the strong.

You cannot help the wage earner by pulling down the wage payer.

You cannot further the brotherhood of man by encouraging class hatred.

You cannot keep out of trouble by spending more than you earn.

You cannot build character and courage by taking away a person's initiative and independence.

You cannot help people permanently by doing for them what they could and should do for themselves.

— *Abraham Lincoln*
President
United States of America

Integrity

The quality or state of being complete, whole, unimpaired, sound.

We gain integrity by bringing together three
 elements that make us whole – honesty,
generosity and goodwill.

— *Casey Chaney*

Taking Risk

When duty, challenge or adventure calls you into
uncharted territory, don't be afraid to act. Go!
Go with courage and enthusiasm, and give it your
best effort. At worst, you will have gained
experience and the satisfaction that comes
from having tried.

— *John K. Rye/DRM*

Be Yourself

Recognize your own uniqueness. Allow your
personal pluses to form a distinctiveness that,
surprise, will impress those you wish to emulate.

— *Lynn Henning*

Invictus

Out of the night that covers me,
Black as the Pit from pole to pole,
I thank whatever gods may be
For my unconquerable soul.

In the fell clutch of circumstance
I have not winced nor cried aloud.
Under the bludgeonings of chance
My head is bloody, but unbowed.

Beyond this place of wrath and tears
Looms but the horror of the shade.
And yet the menace of the years
Finds, and shall find me, unafraid.

It matters not how strait the gate,
How charged with punishments the scroll,
I am the master of my fate:
I am the captain of my soul.

— *William Ernest Henley*

Parents' Prayer

Most loving Father, the example of parenthood,
you have entrusted our children to us to bring them
up for you and prepare them for everlasting life.
Assist us with your grace, that we may fulfill this
sacred duty with competence and love. Teach us
what to give and what to withhold. Show us when
to reprove, when to praise and when to be silent.
Make us gentle and considerate, yet firm and
watchful. Keep us from the weakness of indulgence
and the excess of severity. Give us the courage to be
disliked sometimes by our children, when we must
do necessary things that are displeasing in their
eyes. Give us the imagination to enter their world
in order to understand and guide them. Grant us all
the virtues we need to lead them by word and
example in the ways of wisdom and piety. One day,
with them, may we enter into the joys of our true
and lasting home with you in heaven. Amen.

— *Anonymous*

Stress
The confusion created when one's mind overrides
the body's basic desire to choke the living shit out
of some asshole who desperately deserves it.

— *Anonymous*

Today
Father, today is the only day I possess.
Teach me to use it wisely.
Help me to put the past behind me,
to live this one moment as a peace-maker,
a servant of humanity,
doing my own unique part
to reconcile the world to You.
Amen.

— *Anonymous*

Honesty
I have never met nor heard of anyone who could
out-smart honesty.

— *Abraham Lincoln*

Objectivity

"Now tell me *their* side of the issue just as eloquently and persuasively as you've just told yours."

— *Anonymous/DRM*

Count Your Blessings, for . . .

One billion of the world's people live on less than one dollar a day; they are too poor to obtain the caloric intake needed for health, growth and productive work. Three times that number live on less than two dollars a day. One billion people have no access to clean water; two billion have no access to power and three billion no access to sanitation.

— *Fr. Thomas Shutter, quoting*
Data gathered at the turn of the millennium in 2000.

Planning

Begin with the end in mind.

— *Stephen R. Covey*

The Man in the Glass

When you get what you want in your struggle
for self and the world makes you king for a day,
just go to the mirror and look at yourself and see
what that man has to say.

For it isn't your Father or Mother or wife whose
judgment upon you must pass. The fellow whose
verdict counts most in your life is the one staring
back from the glass.

Some people may call you a straight shooting
chum and call you a wonderful guy, but the man
in the glass says you're only a bum if you can't look
him straight in the eye.

He's the fellow to please, never mind all the rest
for he's with you clear to the end. And you have
passed your most dangerous test if the man in the
glass is your friend.

You may face the whole world down the pathway
of life and get pats on the back when you pass,
but your final reward will be heartache and strife
if you've cheated the man in the glass.

— *Harry Holland Upchurch*

Security

Security is mostly a superstition. It does not exist
in nature, nor do the children of men as a whole
experience it. Avoiding danger is no safer in the
long run than outright exposure. Life is either
a daring adventure or nothing.

— Helen Keller

Moment-to-Moment

Let us strive to make the present moment beautiful.

— St. Francis de Sales

Simplification

Our life is frittered away in detail . . . simplify,
simplify.

— Henry David Thoreau

Myself

I have to live with myself, and so,
I want to be fit for myself to know;
I want to be able as days go by
Always to look myself straight in the eye;
I don't want to stand with the setting sun
And hate myself for the things I've done.

I don't want to keep on a closet shelf
A lot of secrets about myself,
And fool myself as I come and go
Into thinking that nobody else will know
The kind of a man I really am;
I don't want to dress myself up in sham.

I want to go out with my head erect,
I want to deserve all men's respect;
But here in the struggle for fame and pelf,
I want to be able to like myself.
I don't want to think as I come and go
That I'm bluster and bluff and empty show.

I never can hide myself from me,
I see what others may never see,
I know what others may never know,
I never can fool myself — and so,
Whatever happens, I want to be
Self-respecting and conscience free.

— *Edgar A. Guest*

God and Love
God is Love.
And where *true* love is found,
God is always there.

— Church Hymn

Life
Nobody escapes the human condition. Each of us is
dealt some bad cards along the way. Success in life
is measured by how we handle them.

— DRM

Conviction
Cherish your visions; cherish your ideals; cherish
the music that stirs in your heart, the beauty that
forms in your mind, the loveliness that drapes
your purest thoughts, for out of them will grow
all delightful conditions, all heavenly environment;
of these, if you but remain true to them, your world
will at last be built.

— James Allen, "As A Man Thinketh"

Kindergarten

Most of what I really need to know about how
to live, and what to do, and how to be, I learned
in kindergarten. These are the things I learned:

Share everything.
Play fair.
Don't hit people.
Put things back where you found them.
Clean up your own mess.
Don't take things that aren't yours.
Say you're sorry when you hurt somebody. . . .
      Warm cookies and milk are good for you.
Live a balanced life – learn some and think some
      and draw and paint and sing and dance and play
      and work every day some.
Take a nap every afternoon.
When you go out into the world, watch for traffic,
      hold hands and stick together.
Be aware of wonder. Remember the little seed in
      the Styrofoam cup: The roots go down and the
      plant goes up and nobody knows how or why,
      but we are all like that.
Goldfish and hamsters and white mice and even the
      little seed in the Styrofoam cup – they all die.
      So do we.

                                    — *Robert Fulghum*
"All I Really Need To Know I Learned In Kindergarten"

Experience
Nothing ever becomes real until it is experienced.

— Keats

Trust
One day a man told me a secret.
Awhile later I whispered it in the ear of a friend.

The man came back to me, later, after the secret
had been retold to him. And he said to me,

"I told *you* the secret because I did not trust
him with it.

From that day I've looked at trust differently.

— Anonymous

Mental Focus
Think pure thoughts.

— Len Darby

Tone of Voice

It's not so much what you say,
as the manner in which you say it.
It's not so much the language you use,
as the tone in which you convey it.

"Come here!" I sharply said,
and the child cowered and wept.
"Come here," I said – he looked and smiled,
and straight to my lap he crept.

Words may be mild and fair,
but the tone may pierce like a dart.
Words may be soft as the summer air,
but the tone may break my heart.

For words come from the mind,
grow by study and art,
but tone leaps from the inner self,
revealing the state of the heart.

Whether you know it or not,
whether you mean or care,
gentleness, kindness, love and hate,
envy, and anger are there.

Then, would you quarrels avoid,
and peace and love rejoice?
Keep anger not only out of your words –
Keep it out of your voice.

— *Anonymous*

Reason for Being

I don't know how to say it, but some how it
    seems to me
That maybe we are stationed where God wants
    us to be;
That the little place I'm filling is the reason for
    my birth,
And just to do the work I do, He sent me down
    to earth.
If God had wanted otherwise, I reckon
    He'd have made
Me just a little different, of a worse or better grade;
And since God knows and understands all things
    of land and sea,
I fancy that He placed me here, just where
    He wanted me.
Sometimes I get to thinking, as my labors I review,
That I should like a higher place with greater
    things to do;
But I come to the conclusion, when the envying
    is stilled
The post to which God sent me is the post
    He wanted filled.

So, I plod along and struggle in the hope, when
    the day is through,
That I'm really necessary to the things God
    wants to do;
And there isn't any service I can give, which
    I should scorn,
For it may be just the reason God allowed that
    I be born.

              — *Anonymous*

Prayer of Thanks

O tender Father,
you gave me more, much more
than I ever thought to ask for.

I realize that our human desires
can never really match
what You long to give us.

Thanks,
and again thanks, O Father,
for having granted my petitions,
and that which I never realized
I needed or petitioned.

              — *St. Catherine of Siena*

Ideas

A mind stretched to a new idea never goes back
to its original dimensions.

> — *Oliver Wendell Holmes*

Friend

A faithful friend is a sturdy shelter; he who finds
one finds a treasure.

> — *Sir 6:14*

Business "Management"

You *manage* things. You *lead* people.

> — *DRM*

Restful Sleep

To carry care to bed is to sleep with a pack on
your back.

> — *Haliburton*

Tactical Advice
Do not hunt partridges with a band of music.
— *"Safe Methods of Business"*, © *1886*

Can Do
If I walk in the room, I'm going to solve
whatever's there, but I don't know how.
— *Sparky Anderson*

Love
To love another person is to see the face of God.
— *Les Miserables, the Musical*

Career Planning
The price to stay is higher than the price to
get there.
EDS Leadership Conference

You and Them

People are often unreasonable, illogical, and
self-centered;
Forgive them anyway.

If you are kind, people may accuse you of selfish,
ulterior motives;
Be kind anyway.

If you are successful, you will win some false friends
and some true enemies;
Succeed anyway.

If you are honest and frank, people may cheat you;
Be honest and frank anyway.

What you spend years building, someone could
destroy overnight;
Build anyway.

If you find serenity and happiness, they may be
jealous;
Be happy anyway.

The good you do today, people will often forget
tomorrow;
Do good anyway.

Give the world the best you have,
and it may never be enough;
Give the world the best you've got anyway.

You see, in the final analysis, it is between you
and God;
It is never between you and them anyway.

— *Mother Teresa*

Raising Children
It is not enough for parents to nourish only the
bodies of their children; even animals do this.
They must also nourish their *souls* in grace,
in virtue and in God's holy commandments.
— *St. Catherine of Siena*

Leaders
A leader is someone others follow.
— *EDS Leadership Conference*

Anonymity

The work an unknown good man or woman has
done is like a vein of water flowing hidden
underground, secretly making the ground green.

— *Thomas Carlyle*

Success

True success is overcoming the fear of becoming
successful.

— *Paul Sweeney*

Today

Look to this day . . .
For yesterday is but a dream,
And tomorrow is only a vision.
But today well-lived
Makes every yesterday
A dream of happiness,
And every tomorrow
A vision of hope.

— *from the Sanskrit*

Where Credit Belongs

It is not the critic who counts, not the man who points out how the strong man stumbled, or where the doer of deeds could have done them better. The credit belongs to the man who is actually in the arena; whose face is marred by dust and sweat and blood; who strives valiantly; who errs and comes short again and again; who knows the great enthusiasms, the great devotions; who spends himself in a worthy cause; who, at the best knows in the end the triumph of high achievement; and who, at the worst if he fails, at least fails while daring greatly.

— *President Theodore Roosevelt*

Attitude

The contrast between ordinary and great living is the difference between what a person is required to do to exist, and what they feel they can and must do to be their best self. The margin of life is the difference between what they are, and what they might become if they used their potential abilities.

— *Dr. G. Ernest Thomas*

Safely Home

I am home in Heaven, dear ones;
Oh, so happy and so bright!
There is perfect joy and beauty
In this everlasting light.

All the pain and grief is over,
Every restless tossing passed;
I am now at peace forever,
Safely home in Heaven at last.

Did you wonder I so calmly
Trod the valley of the shade?
Oh! but Jesus' love illuminated
Every dark and fearful glade.

And He came Himself to meet me
In the way so hard to tread;
And with Jesus' arm to lean on,
Could I have one doubt or dread?

Then you must not grieve so sorely,
For I love you dearly still;
Try to look beyond earth's shadows,
Pray to trust our Father's Will.

There is work still waiting for you,
So you must not idly stand;
Do it now, while life remaineth –
You can rest in Jesus' land.

When that work is all completed,
He will gently call you Home;
Oh, the rapture of that meeting,
Oh, the joy to see you come!

— *Anonymous*

Failure

I have not failed. I've just found 10,000 ways
that won't work.

— *Thomas Edison*

Friends

A friend is someone who knows the song in your
heart and can sing it back to you when you have
forgotten the words.

— *Anonymous*

Faith

My Lord God,
I have no idea where I am going,
I do not see the road ahead of me.
I cannot know where it will end.
Nor do I really know myself,
And the fact that I think that I am following your
     will does not mean that I am actually doing so.

But I believe that the desire to please you does
     in fact please you.
And I hope I have that desire in all I am doing.
I hope that I will never do anything apart from
     that desire.
And I know that if I do this,
you will lead me by the right road, though I may
     know nothing about it.

Therefore, I will trust you always, though I may
     seem to be lost in the shadow of death.
I will not fear, for you are ever with me, and
     you will never leave me to face my perils alone.
Amen.

— *Thomas Merton*

Birth

A baby is God's opinion that the world should
go on.

> — *Carl Sandburg*

Peace of Mind

Nothing can bring you peace but yourself.
Nothing can bring you peace but the triumph of
principles.

To believe your own thought, to believe that
what is true for you in your private heart is true
for all men – that is genius.

> — *Ralph Waldo Emerson*

Human Nature

All human beings are inherently hedonistic.
When given a choice, a person will always choose
what makes him feel good.

> — *MBA Professor*

Life
Shit Happens!

— *Bumper Sticker*

Priorities
There is an appointed time for everything . . . a time
to weep, and a time to laugh, a time to mourn, and
a time to dance.

— *Eccl 3:1,4*

Salvaging Good From Bad
Making "lemonade from lemons"

— *Diane O'Brien*

Teamwork
Men work together, whether they work
together or apart.

— *Robert Frost*

Productivity

If you need a job done, give it to a busy wo/man.

— *Anonymous*

Success

At age 4, success is not peeing in your pants.
At age 12, success is having friends.
At age 16, success is having a driver's license.
At age 20, success is having sex.
At age 35, success is having money.
At age 50, success is having money.
At age 60, success is having sex.
At age 70, success is having a driver's license.
At age 75, success is having friends.
At age 80, success is not peeing in your pants.

— *Anonymous*

Murphy's Law

If anything can go wrong, it will.

— *Edsel Murphy*

Money

Spend it. It's the only reason you work for it.

— *John P. Prodin, Jr.*

Humility

Do not let me hear
Of the wisdom of old men, but rather of their folly,
Their fear of fear and frenzy, their fear of possession,
Of belonging to another, or to others, or to God.

The only wisdom we can hope to acquire
Is the wisdom of humility: humility is endless.

— *T.S. Eliot, Four Quartets*

Kids

Kids are God's way of telling us there are others
in the world more important than us.

— *Norman Mailer*

The Future
The best thing about the future is that it comes only one day at a time.

— *Anonymous*

Gullibility
There's a sucker born every minute.

— *P. T. Barnum*

Dangerous Mouths
"You got to keep your eye on his mouth. The mouth is the most dangerous part of a person. A guy can do more damage with his mouth than Muhammad Ali with his fists. You gotta be a mouth watcher."

— *New York Cab Driver*

Habits of Others
Nothing so needs reforming as other people's habits.

— *Mark Twain*

Psalm 23

The Lord is My Shepherd, I shall not want.

In verdant pastures He gives me repose.

Beside restful waters He leads me.

He refreshes my soul.

He guides me in the right paths for his name's sake.

Even though I walk in the dark valley I fear no evil,
> for you are at my side with your rod and staff
> that give me comfort.

You spread the table before me in the presence
> of my enemies.

You anoint my head with oil;
> my cup overflows.

Surely goodness and love will follow me
> all the days of my life,

And I will dwell in the house of the Lord forever.

— *David*

Enduring Difficulties

Harsh winds strong trees grow.

— *Anonymous*

Come Holy Spirit
Come Holy Spirit; fill the hearts of your faithful.
And kindle in us the fires of your love.
Send forth your spirit, and they shall be created.
And you shall renew the face of the earth.

Lord, by the light of the Holy Spirit you have
taught the hearts of your faithful. In the same
Spirit help us to relish what is right and always
rejoice in your consolation. We ask this through
Christ our Lord. Amen.

— Anonymous

Leadership
If you meet the employees of a company, you don't
have to meet the guy that's running it.

— Sparky Anderson

Facts
Generally the theories we believe we call facts,
and the facts we disbelieve we call theories.

— Felix Cohen

A Christmas Prayer

Loving Father,
help us remember the birth of Jesus,
that we may share in the song of the angels,
the gladness of the shepherds,
and worship of the wise men.

Close the door of hate and open the door of
love all over the world.
Let kindness come with every gift and good
desires with every greeting.
Deliver us from evil by the blessing that Christ
brings,
and teach us to be merry with clear hearts.

May the Christmas morning make us happy to be
thy children,
and Christmas evening bring us to our beds with
grateful thoughts,
forgiving and forgiven,
for Jesus' sake.
Amen.

— *Robert Louis Stevenson*

By Our Actions
We become just by performing just actions,
temperate by performing temperate actions,
brave by performing brave actions.

— Aristotle

Which Problem?
It is usually easier to ask for forgiveness than
to seek permission.

— Frank J. Babel

Faith
If God brings you to it - He will bring you
through it.

— Anonymous

Wisdom
Wisdom is having a lot to say – and not saying it.

— Anonymous

Challenges

Don't be afraid to take a big step. You can't cross
a chasm in two small jumps.

— *David Lloyd George*

Leadership Effect

An institution is the lengthened shadow of one man
(or woman).

— *Ralph Waldo Emerson*

Selling

People like doing business with people who like
them and are like them.

— *Anonymous*

Excellence

Caring more than others think is wise.
Risking more than others think is safe.
Dreaming more than others think is practical.
Expecting more than others think is possible.

— *Anonymous*

Mediocrity
Mediocrity is excellence to the mediocre.

— Anonymous

Being Big
Being a "big" person is no small task.

— DRM

Law of Open Options
Nothing is impossible for people who don't have
to do it themselves.

— Anonymous

Right v. Wrong
If it's almost right, it's wrong.

— Don Oberg

Decisions
Choose which problem you're willing to live with.

— EDS Leadership Conference

The Gift

Having been tenant long to a rich lord,
Not thriving, I resolved to be bold,
And make a suit unto him, to afford
A new small-rented lease, and cancel the old.

In heaven at his manor I him sought;
They told me there that he was lately gone
About some land, which he had dearly bought
Long since on earth, to take possession.

I straight returned, and knowing his great birth,
Sought him accordingly in great resorts;
In cities, theaters, gardens, parks, and courts;
At length I heard a ragged noise and mirth
Of thieves and murderers; there I him espied,
Who straight, "Your suit is granted," said,
and died.

— *George Herbert*

Success
Avoiding failure isn't the same as achieving success.
— *Chinese Fortune Cookie*

Loving Life
My life has no purpose, no direction, no aim,
no meaning, and yet I'm happy. I can't figure it out.
What am I doing right?
— *Charles Schulz*

Experience
Experience is not what happens to you. It is
what you do with what happens to you.
— *Aldous Huxley*

Politics
Politics is the art of looking for trouble, finding it,
misdiagnosing it and then misapplying the
wrong remedies.
— *Groucho Marx*

Desiderata

Go placidly amid the noise and the haste, and remember what peace there may be in silence.

As far as possible, without surrender, be on good terms with all persons.

Speak your truth quietly and clearly; and listen to others, even the dull and ignorant; they too have their story.

Avoid loud and aggressive persons; they are vexatious to the spirit.

If you compare yourself with others you may become vain and bitter; for always there will be greater and lesser persons than yourself.

Enjoy your achievements as well as your plans. Keep interested in your own career, however humble; it is a real possession in the changing fortunes of time.

Exercise caution in your business affairs; for the world is full of trickery. But let this not blind you to what virtue there is; many persons strive for high ideals; and everywhere life is full of heroism.

Be yourself. Especially do not feign affection.
Neither be cynical about love; for in the face of all
aridity and disenchantment it is as perennial
as the grass.

Take kindly the counsel of the years, gracefully
surrendering the things of youth. Nurture strength
of spirit to shield you in sudden misfortune But do
not distress yourself with imaginings. Many fears
are born of fatigue and loneliness.

Beyond a wholesome discipline, be gentle with
yourself.

You are a child of the universe no less than the trees
and the stars; you have a right to be here.
And whether or not it is clear to you,
no doubt the universe is unfolding as it should.

Therefore, be at peace with God, whatever you
conceive Him to be. And whatever your labors and
aspirations in the noisy confusion of life, keep pace
with your soul.

With all its sham, drudgery and broken dreams, it is
still a beautiful world.

Be cheerful. Strive to be happy.

— *Max Ehrmann*

Prayer of Self Abandonment

Father, I abandon myself into Your hands;
do with me whatever You will.
Whatever you may do I thank You:
I am ready for all. I accept all.

Let only Your will be done in me,
and in all Your creatures.
I wish no more than this O Lord.
Into Your hands I commend my soul:
I offer it to You with all the love of my heart,
for I love You, Lord, and so need to give myself,
to surrender myself into your hands,
without reserve, and with boundless confidence,
for you are my Father.

— *Brother Charles de Foucauld*

Love

Love, and do what you will. If you are silent,
be silent out of love. If you speak, speak out of love.
If you censure, censure out of love. If you forbear,
forbear out of love. But love in your heart. Nothing
but good can spring from that source.

— *St. Augustine*

Americans

To a greater or a lesser extent, we are all confidence
men, actors playing the characters of our own
invention and hoping that the audience – fortunately
consisting of impostors as fanciful or synthetic as
ourselves – will accept the performance at par value
and suspend the judgments of ridicule.

— *Lewis H. Lapham*

Trickle-Down Leadership

Over time subordinates tend to become carbon
copies of their chief.

— *Anonymous*

Dreaming

The dreamers are the saviors of the world.
Dream lofty dreams, and as you dream, so shall
you become.

— *James Allen, "As A Man Thinketh"*

Age
Age is a question of mind over matter. If you
don't mind, it don't matter.

— *Satchel Paige*

Employees
At the end of the day we're all subject to the
wisdom of our superiors.

— *DRM*

Vision and Action
Vision without action is merely a dream.
Action without vision just passes the time.
Vision with action can change the world.

— *Joel Arthur Barker*

Effectiveness
If what you are doing is not value-added, it should
be waste elimination. If it is neither, then it is
a waste.

— *Jim McKelvey*

Slow Me Down Lord

Slow me down, Lord! Slow me down!
Ease the pounding of my heart by the quieting
of my mind.
Steady my hurried pace with a vision of the eternal
reach of time.
Give me, amidst the confusion of my day, the calmness
of the everlasting hills.
Break the tensions of my nerves with the soothing
music of the singing streams that live in my memory.
Help me to know the magical restoring power of sleep.
Teach me the art of taking minute vacations.
Of slowing down to look at a flower; to pat a dog;
to watch a spider build a web; to smile at a child;
or to read from a good book.
Remind me each day of the fable of the hare and
tortoise, that I may know that the race is not always
to the swift – that there is more to life than
increasing its speed.
Let me look upward into the towering oak and know
that it grew great and strong because it grew slowly
and well.
Slow me down, Lord, and inspire me to send my roots
deep into the soil of life's enduring values, that I may
grow toward the stars of greater destiny.

— *Wilfred A. Peterson*

Good Enough

My son beware of "good enough,"
It isn't made of sterling stuff;
It's something any man can do,
It marks the many from the few,
It has no merit to the eye,
It's something any man can buy,
Its name is but a sham and bluff,
For it is never "good enough."

With "good enough" the shirkers stop
In every factory and shop;
With "good enough" the failures rest
And lose to men who give their best;
With "good enough" the car breaks down
And men fall short of high renown.
My son, remember and be wise,
In "good enough", disaster lies.

With "good enough" have ships been wrecked,
The forward march of armies checked,
The great buildings burned and fortunes lost;
Nor can the world compute the cost
In life and money it has paid
Because at "good enough" men stayed.
Who stops at "good enough" shall find
Success has left him far behind.

There is no "good enough" that's short
Of what you can do and you ought.
The flaw, which may escape the eye
And temporarily get by,
Shall weaken underneath the strain
And wreck the ship or car or train.
For this is true of men and stuff –
Only the best is "good enough."

— Edgar A. Guest

Goodness

We can be excused for not being always gay,
for we are not masters of gaiety so as to have it
when we wish. But we cannot be excused for
not being good, agreeable, and gracious, because
this is always in the power of our will.

— St. Francis de Sales

Compensation

If you concentrate on the *work* and forget about
the *money*, you'll get more of the latter.

— John Law/DRM

Ladder of Success

Kites rise highest against the wind – not with it.

— *Winston Churchill*

Living

Work as if you don't need money,
Dance as if nobody's watching,
Love as if you'll never get hurt.

— *Anonymous*

Words Spoken

It is not what enters one's mouth that defiles
one . . . the things that come out of the mouth come
from the heart, and they defile. For from the heart
came evil thoughts, murder, adultery, unchastity,
theft, false witness, and blasphemy. These are
what defile a person, but to eat with unwashed
hands does not defile.

— *Mt 15:11, 18-20*

Mindset

Happiness, like unhappiness, is a proactive choice.

— *Stephen R. Covey*

Managing

The toughest thing about coaching is you have
to lie at your players.

— *Sparky Anderson*

Life

Our life is what our thoughts make of it.

— *Marcus Aurelius*

Fads

If everyone else is doing it, you're already too late.
Do something else.

— *DRM*

Sonnet CXVI

Let me not to the marriage of true minds
Admit impediments. Love is not love
Which alters when it alteration finds,
Or bends with the remover to remove:
O no! It is an ever-fixed mark
That looks on tempests and is never shaken;
It is the star to every wandering bark,
Whose worth's unknown, although his height
be taken.
Love's not Time's fool, though rosy lips and cheeks
Within his bending sickle's compass come:
Love alters not with his brief hours and weeks,
    But bears it out even to the edge of doom.
    If this be error and upon me proved,
I never writ, nor no man ever loved.

— William Shakespeare

Choosing Friends and Colleagues
It is hard to fly like an eagle when you're
surrounded by turkeys.

— Anonymous

Healthy Pride

When I look at Your heavens, the work of
Your fingers, the moon and the stars that you have
established; what are human beings that You are
mindful of them, mortals that You care for them?
Yet You have made them a little lower than God,
and crowned them with glory and honor.

— Psalm 8:3-5

Greatness

Most people talk about *others*.
Some people talk about *things*.
Great people discuss *ideas*.

— Anonymous

Persistence

It is possible to move a mountain by carrying away
small stones.

— Chinese Proverb

Now Is The Time

Out of the vast universe,
in the entire history of time,
we have come together
to spend these moments
and the balance of our days
with each other.

Not knowing our time remaining
or what tomorrow may provide,
we have this rare chance
to learn to love one another –
sensitively and delicately,
fully and deeply.

With our brief span passing
at an ever faster pace,
we can let the days
slip through our grasp
or we can remember that
these are our moments now.

— *Robert Connors Hellrung*

The Customer

Because the customer has a need,
We have a job to do.

Because the customer has a choice,
We must be the better choice.

Because the customer has sensibilities,
We must be considerate.

Because the customer has an urgency,
We must be quick.

Because the customer is unique,
We must be flexible.

Because the customer has high expectations,
We must excel.

Because the customer has influence,
We have the hope of more customers.

Because of the customer,
We exist!

— *Anonymous*

Longevity
A light heart lives long.

— Shakespeare

Values
A hundred years from now, it will not matter what
my bank account was, the sort of house I lived in,
or the kind of car I drove, but the world may be
different because I was important in the life
of a child.

— Anonymous

Will
Confront your fears.

— Tom Henderson

Faith
I believe in the sun even when it is not shining.
I believe in love even when I do not have it.
I believe in God even when He is silent.

— Anonymous/Antonina

Strategy

In business as in bridge, a single peek is worth
a thousand finesses.

— Orval Operthauser

Business Management

Honest, intelligent, industrious Management is
crucial. It cannot be faked. You either have it
or you don't. Without it the entity will eventually
fail, regardless of its history.

— DRM

Enthusiasm

Nothing worthwhile is ever accomplished without
enthusiasm.

— Mr. Wrigley quoting his Grandfather

The Future

We should all be concerned about the future because
we have to spend the rest of our lives there.

— Charles Kettering

Boy Scout Oath

On my honor I will do my best
To do my duty to God and my country, and
To obey the Scout Law;
To help other people at all times;
To keep myself physically strong,
mentally awake, and morally straight.

— *Sir Robert Baden-Powell, 1909*

Scout Law

A Scout is:

Trustworthy

Loyal

Helpful

Friendly

Courteous

Kind

Obedient

Cheerful

Thrifty

Brave

Clean

Reverent

— *Sir Robert Baden-Powell, 1909*

Corporate Rigor Mortis

"The management regrets that it has come to
their attention that workers dying on the job are
failing to fall down. This practice must stop,
as it becomes impossible to distinguish between
death and the natural movement of the staff.
Any employee found dead in an upright position
will be dropped from the payroll."

— Anonymous

Action and Reflection

Let every word be the fruit of action and reflection.

Reflection alone, without action or tending toward
it, is mere theory, adding its weight when we are
overloaded with it already.

Action alone without reflection is busy pointlessly.

Honor the Word eternal and speak to make
a new world possible.

— Dom Helder Camara
Archbishop of Olinda-Recife, Brazil

Ideas

The right idea
Offered at the right time
To the right people
In the right way
Is a thing of great power.

— Anonymous

Healing

You who dwell in the shelter of the Most High,
who abide in the shadow of the Almighty,
Say to the Lord, "My refuge and fortress,
my God in whom I trust."

God will rescue you from the fowler's snare,
from the destroying plague,
With his pinions he will cover you, and under
his wings you shall take refuge.
God's faithfulness is a protecting shield.

You shall not fear the terror of the night,
nor the arrow that flies by day,
Nor the pestilence that roams in darkness,
nor the plaque that ravages at noon.

Though a thousand fall at your side,
ten thousand at your right hand,
near you it shall not come.
You need simply watch;
the punishment of the wicked you will see.

You have the Lord for your refuge;
you have made the Most High your stronghold.
No evil shall befall you,
no affliction come near your tent.

For God commands the angels
to guard you in all your ways.
With their hands they shall support you,
lest you strike your foot against the stone.

You shall tread upon the asp and the viper,
trample the lion and the dragon.
Whoever clings to me I will deliver;
whoever knows my name I will set on high.

All who call upon me I will answer;
I will be with them in distress;
I will deliver them and give them honor.
With length of days I will satisfy them
and show them my saving power.

— *Psalm 91*

I Am There

Do you need me?

I am there.

You cannot see Me, yet I am the light you see by.

You cannot hear Me, yet I speak through your voice.

You cannot feel Me, yet I am the power at work in
your hands.

I am at work, though you do not understand My ways.

I am at work, though you do not recognize My works.

I am not strange visions. I am not mysteries.

Only in absolute stillness, beyond self, can you know
Me as I am, and then but as a feeling and a faith.

Yet I am there. Yet I hear. Yet I answer.

When you need Me, I am there.

Even if you deny Me, I am there.

Even when you feel most alone, I am there.

Even in your fears, I am there.

Even in your pain, I am there.

I am there when you pray and when you do not pray.

I am in you, and you are in Me.

Only in your mind can you feel separate from Me,
for only in your mind are the mists of "yours"
and "mine."

Yet only with your mind can you know Me and
experience Me.

Empty your heart of empty fears.

When you get yourself out of the way, I am there.

You can of yourself do nothing, but I can do all.

And I am in all.

Though you may not see the good, good is there,
for I am there.

I am there because I have to be, because I am.

Only in Me does the world have meaning; only out
of Me does the world take form; only because
of Me does the world go forward.

I am the law on which the movement of the stars
and the growth of living cells are founded.

I am the love that is the law's fulfilling. I am
assurance. I am peace. I am oneness. I am the law
that you can live by. I am the love that you can
cling to. I am your assurance. I am your peace.
I am one with you. I am.

Though you fail to find Me, I do not fail you.

Though your faith in Me is unsure, My faith in you
never wavers, because I know you, because
I love you.

Beloved, I am there.

— *James Dillet Freeman*

Success

A successful life is mainly just a matter of putting
one foot in *front* of the other, hour-by-hour,
day-by-day, year-by-year.

— *DRM*

Psalm 72

O God of love,
Grant to your children and servants the grace
To represent you effectively in the world.
Give us the courage
To put lives on the line
In communicating life and truth
To all your creatures
Wherever they may be found.

Where there is injustice,
May we diagnose its cause
And discover its cure.
Where there is bigotry,
Teach us how to love
And how to encourage others to love.

Where there is poverty,
Help us to share the wealth
That has come from your hand.
Where there is war and violence,
May we be peacemakers that lead people
To Your eternal peace.

Help us, O God, to become what you
Have destined and empowered us to become
Where there is darkness,
May we become the rays of your sun
That banish the gloom of lonely lives.

Where there is drought
Let us be like fresh showers
That turn the barren deserts into green meadows.
Where there is ugliness and distortion,
Enable us to portray the beauty and order
Of your will and purpose.

Great God, You are in our world,
Your majesty is reflected
In your creation about us.
But there are multitudes that do not
Feel your concern or
Acknowledge your will.

Is it because your servants have failed
To carry out your command and commission
That we have yet to sense
The significance of our salvation
And the purpose of our mission?

Forbid, O God
That we be deaf to the cries of the poor
And indifferent to those who have needs.
May we identify with those who are oppressed
And help to bear the burdens
Of those who suffer about us.
May we hear your voice of concern
And feel your loving touch
Through your servants who are in this world
To manifest you to those about them.

The glory is yours, O God,
And we shall praise your name
And celebrate your cause together.

> — *Adapted from "Psalms Now" by Leslie Brandt &*
> *Corita Kent*

Tomorrow

What'er there be of sorrow
I'll put off till tomorrow,
And then when tomorrow comes,
Why then
T'will be today and joy again.

> — *Anonymous*

Around the Corner

Around the corner I have a friend,
In this great city that has no end.
Yet days go by and weeks rush on,
And before I know it, a year is gone.
And I never see my old friend's face;
For life is a swift and terrible race.
He knows I like him just as well
As in the days when I rang his bell.
And he rang mine. We were younger then —
And now we are busy, tired men —
Tired with trying to make a name.
"Tomorrow," I say, "I will call on Jim,
Just to show that I'm thinking of him."
But tomorrow comes — and tomorrow goes;
And the distance between us grows and grows.
Around the corner! Yet miles away. . .
"Here's a telegram, sir."
"Jim died today."
And that's what we get — and deserve in the end —
Around the corner, a vanished friend.

— *Henson Towne*

Time Management
Deadlines are your friends.

— Dale Dauten

Behavior
Human behavior is always rational . . . from the point of view of the behaving person.

— MBA Professor

Love is . . .
Everything a heart can hold,
But only for a minute!
For to love is to give
And to give is to know
Joy, peace and satisfaction.

— Anonymous

As Others Thinketh
You cannot control and are not responsible for what another person *thinks*.

— DRM

Normal Day

Normal Day, let me be aware of the
treasure you are. Let me learn
from you, love you, savor you, bless
you, before you depart.

Let me not pass you by in quest of some
rare and perfect tomorrow. Let me
hold you while I may, for it will not
always be so.

One day I shall dig my fingers into the
earth, or bury my face in the pillow,
or stretch myself taut, or raise my
hands to the sky, and want more than
all the world: your return.

— *Mary Jean Irion*
"Yes, World: A Mosaic of Meditation"

About the Sources

Through the years as each of the clippings and mental notes that make up this work was collected, I recorded the source. Then, as I went about transforming the collection into this book, I did the following:

If the entry was clipped from a printed publication or gleaned from an audio source that identified the original author, he or she was credited with it. If no original author was noted, the source is listed as Anonymous. If the learning came as the result of a personal contact, then I listed the person that I recalled first hearing or reading it from as the source. If I could not recall from whom I first learned it, then the source is listed as Anonymous.

Despite a sincere effort to do it correctly. I undoubtedly made a few mistakes in ascribing the sources. For these I apologize.

Additionally, some sources are noticeable by their absence — my mother and father, for example, and other close friends, relatives and business associates. The fact that they are not listed, is certainly not indicative of their contribution to my beliefs and values. To the contrary, my formation was influenced greatly by individuals whose names do not appear in this work. A great number of contacts and loved ones, including my parents, have taught me and others by their example more than words.

— DRM

Feedback Here

I welcome your comments and questions.
Please send them to me at:

author@prayerandwisdom.com

— or —

Topanga Publishing
PO Box 535
Coloma, MI 49038-0535

Additional copies can be ordered by
downloading the form found at:

www.topangapublishing.com

— DRM

Index of
Titles and Sources

M

N

S

Y

Z